# The Tallgrass Prairie Center Guide to
# Seed and Seedling Identification in the Upper Midwest

T0021623

A BUR OAK GUIDE

# The Tallgrass Prairie Center Guide to
# Seed and Seedling Identification in the Upper Midwest

BY DAVE WILLIAMS

ILLUSTRATED BY BRENT BUTLER

Published for the Tallgrass Prairie Center
by the University of Iowa Press, Iowa City

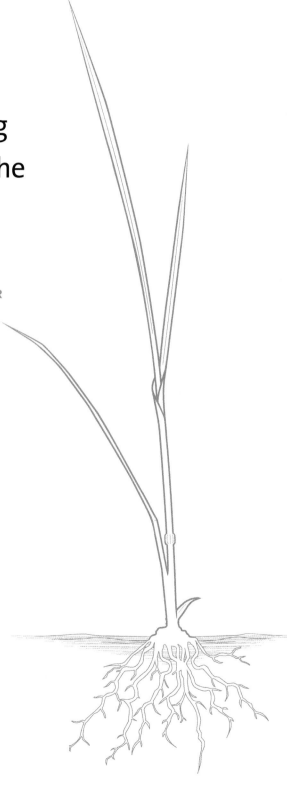

University of Iowa Press, Iowa City 52242
Copyright © 2010 by the Tallgrass Prairie Center
www.uiowapress.org
Printed in the United States of America

Design by April Leidig-Higgins

No part of this book may be reproduced or used
in any form or by any means without permission
in writing from the publisher. All reasonable steps
have been taken to contact copyright holders of
material used in this book. The publisher would be
pleased to make suitable arrangements with any
whom it has not been possible to reach.

The University of Iowa Press is a member of Green
Press Initiative and is committed to preserving
natural resources.

Printed on acid-free paper

Library of Congress Cataloging-in-Publication Data
Williams, Dave (David Wayne), 1961–
The Tallgrass Prairie Center guide to seed and seed-
ling identification in the Upper Midwest / by Dave
Williams; illustrated by Brent Butler. — 1st ed.
    p.   cm. — (A Bur Oak guide)
Includes index.
ISBN-13: 978-1-58729-902-5 (pbk.)
ISBN-10: 1-58729-902-x (pbk.)
    1. Prairie plants — Seeds — Middle West —
Identification.   2. Forbs — Seeds — Middle West
— Identification.   3. Grasses — Seeds — Middle
West — Identification.   4. Seedlings — Middle
West — Identification.   I. Butler, Brent, 1978–
II. Tallgrass Prairie Center.   III. Title.   IV. Title:
Guide to seed and seedling identification in the
Upper Midwest.   V. Series: Bur Oak guide.
QK128.W55   2010
581.7'440978 — dc22              2010000528

To my wife, Maureen,
for her encouragement, patience,
and editorial advice

and to Rob, Clair, and Kayee
for their willingness to venture
into wild places with Dad
— Dave Williams

To my late grandfather, James Butler,
for showing me the beauty of Iowa
roadsides on our summer trips,

and to my father-in-law, Bob Athen,
whose conservation efforts continue
to inspire me
— Brent Butler

# CONTENTS

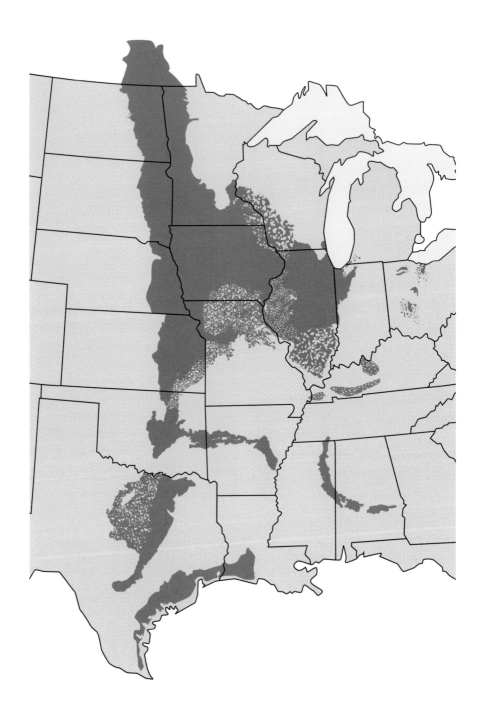

When settlers crossed the tallgrass prairie, they were greeted by a vibrant, seemingly endless landscape of wildflowers, grasses, and sedges. These plants created a mosaic of colors and textures that extended from Canada to Texas and from the eastern Dakotas to parts of Indiana and Ohio. The tallgrass prairie was one of the most diverse ecosystems on our planet. Over the eons, its plants adapted to severe cold winters and hot dry summers to leave a legacy of the most productive soils on earth. Today, the tallgrass prairie has been reduced to small, isolated fragments found in rights-of-way, cemeteries, and areas too steep, rocky, or awkward to farm.

The goal of this guide is twofold. First, it should provide interesting information about the depth and breadth of native forbs and grasses of the prairie to encourage readers to consider using tallgrass prairie seed and/or live plants for their next planting projects. Second, this guide will aid in the identification of seedling plants as they emerge from the soil.

The definition of a seedling plant is somewhat arbitrary. The challenge for us in writing this guide was to produce seedlings that were close in size and developmental stage to that of field-grown seedlings near the end of their first growing season. To accomplish this, we grew plants in the greenhouse for four to six weeks. A few species such as Canada anemone, Culver's root, and prairie smoke needed a few extra weeks because their seed took longer to germinate and their growth was much slower. Keep in mind that as most plants mature, they undergo a series of morphological changes, and their unique seedling characteristics can appear and disappear in a few short weeks. Seedling identification can be greatly enhanced by watching these early changes as the plants mature.

This guide organizes seedling plants into two groups: forbs and grasses. Associated with each group is a line drawing of a seedling with its most important parts highlighted. Remember those parts, because seedling identification is nothing more than finding them — or not finding them — in a key. Seedlings are therefore grouped by their key characteristics, not by their species or in alphabetical order. There are seven key characteristic groups for forbs and four for grasses, representing seventy-two different species.

To identify an unknown tallgrass prairie seedling, you'll first find its key characteristics, using the appropriate line drawing in conjunction with the guidance provided in the forbs and grasses identification sections on pages 2–3 and 86–87. Sometimes you may need to roll a stem between your fingers or look through a hand lens to find certain details. You'll be guided step by step, through a process of elimination, to that one of the eleven characteristic groups in the book that best fits your unknown seedling. Look through the section where plants with those characteristics are shown until you find the right one. It's that simple!

Red circles and yellow and blue triangles will also aid in seedling identification. The red circle on each full seedling photograph corresponds to the area of the close-up photograph. In addition, small yellow and blue triangles in the close-up correspond to the bullet points marked with the colored triangles. These will help you pinpoint the key characteristics. Also included are line drawings of leaf types, leaf shapes, leaf arrangements, leaf margins, a glossary of botanical terms, and an index of common and scientific names.

We have used *The Vascular Plants of Iowa: An Annotated Checklist and Natural History* by Lawrence J. Eilers and Dean M. Roosa (1994), *An Illustrated Guide to Iowa Prairie Plants* by Paul Christiansen and Mark Müller (1999), and the USDA Natural Resources Conservation Service PLANTS Database at http://plants.usda.gov for species selection and binomial nomenclature. Where the *Flora of North America North of Mexico* and *The Flora of Nebraska* by Robert B. Kaul, David Sutherland, and Steven Rolfsmeier (2007) provide updated nomenclature, we have included the older names in brackets in the index.

We are glad you are interested in the tallgrass prairie, and we hope this guide will deepen your appreciation and awareness of the unique beauty of our natural landscape.

## ABOUT THE PHOTOGRAPHS

Seedlings were photographed by Dave Williams, David O'Shields, and Brent Butler. An 8-megapixel digital Canon Rebel XT camera with a 100mm macro lens attached was used for full seedling photographs. A series of 12, 20, and 36mm extension tubes were attached to the same camera and lens for the close-ups. With some species, multiple seedlings were used to get the very best close-up shots. A tripod and light table were used for all photographs.

## ACKNOWLEDGMENTS

We thank all who provided the consultation, funding, and equipment to complete this guide. The photographic expertise and advice of Jeffery Byrd were invaluable. The very best photographs were a result of David O'Shields's eye for angle, light, and picture clarity. We thank Maureen Collins-Williams and Holly Carver for their editing of multiple manuscript drafts. Many thanks to the University of Northern Iowa's Tallgrass Prairie Center Director Daryl Smith for providing the equipment and allowing us the time to pursue this project. This guide was funded by the United States Department of Agriculture, Natural Resources Conservation Service.

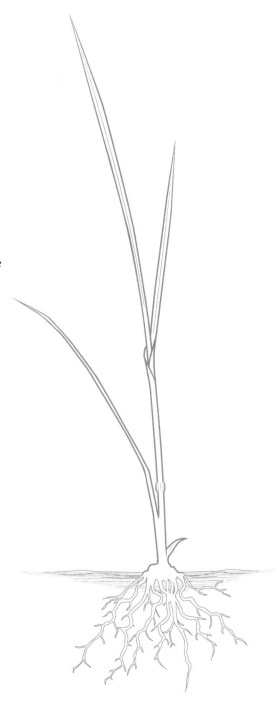

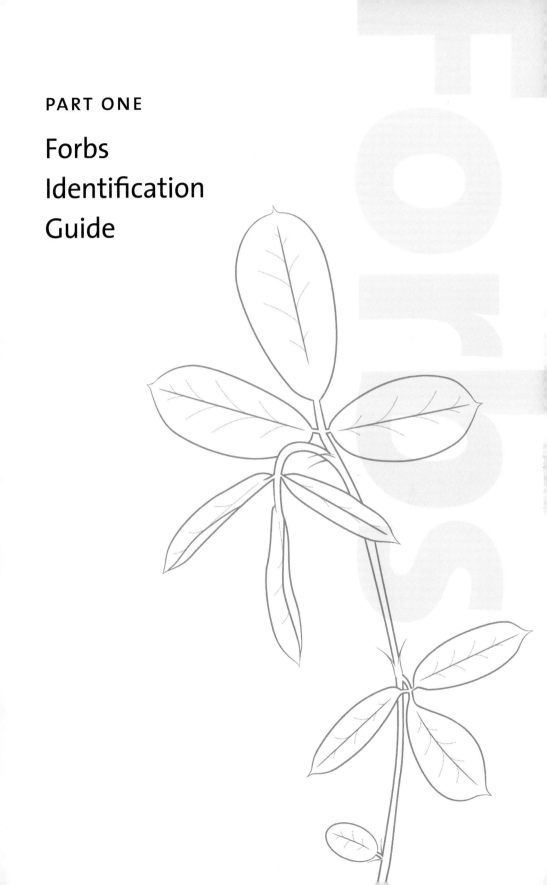

**PART ONE**

# Forbs
# Identification
# Guide

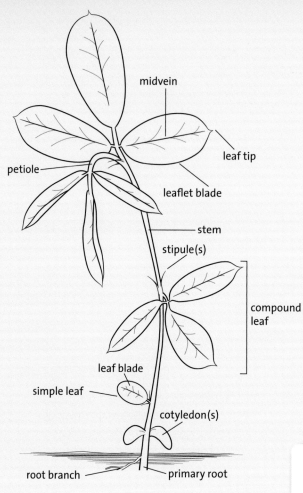

midvein

leaf tip

petiole

leaflet blade

stem

stipule(s)

compound leaf

leaf blade

simple leaf

cotyledon(s)

root branch

primary root

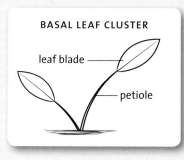

**BASAL LEAF CLUSTER**

leaf blade

petiole

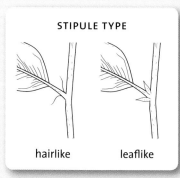

**STIPULE TYPE**

hairlike

leaflike

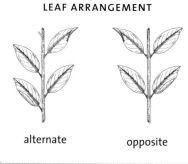

**LEAF ARRANGEMENT**

alternate

opposite

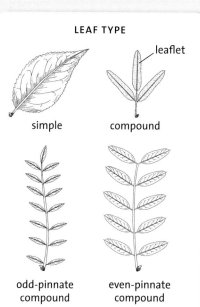

**LEAF TYPE**

leaflet

simple

compound

odd-pinnate
compound

even-pinnate
compound

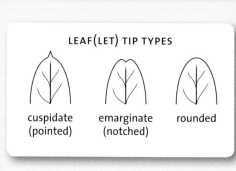

**LEAF(LET) TIP TYPES**

cuspidate
(pointed)

emarginate
(notched)

rounded

Welcome to the forbs identification section. Most prairie plants are perennial and grow slowly (above ground) in the first growing season. Therefore, plant identification may be easier when done in late summer, after seedlings have had the most time to develop. Follow the easy steps below.

1. Start with a visual inspection to determine if your unknown seedling has a stem or is a basal cluster of leaves.
   a. Stem present: go to step 2
   b. Stem absent: go to step 6

2. Roll the stem between your fingers to determine if it is round or has an edge.
   a. Round stem: go to step 3
   b. Edged stem: go to key characteristic group 5, page 38

3. Look for stipules near the base of the petiole (a hand lens may be needed).
   a. Stipules present: go to step 4
   b. Stipules absent: go to step 5

4. Determine if stipules are hairlike or leaflike.
   a. Stipules are hairlike: go to key characteristic group 1, page 4
   b. Stipules are leaflike: go to key characteristic group 2, page 13

5. Determine if leaves are arranged alternate or opposite on the stem.
   a. Alternate leaf arrangement: go to key characteristic group 3, page 19
   b. Opposite leaf arrangement: go to key characteristic group 4, page 26

6. Does the seedling appear grasslike?
   a. No, does not appear grasslike: go to key characteristic group 6, page 49
   b. Yes, appears grasslike: go to key characteristic group 7, page 74

# Forbs:
## Key Characteristic Group 1

Round stem, hairlike stipules,
alternate leaves

Leadplant, *Amorpha canescens*

New Jersey tea, *Ceanothus americanus*

Purple prairie clover, *Dalea purpurea*

Round-headed bush clover,
*Lespedeza capitata*

Showy tick trefoil, *Desmodium canadense*

White prairie clover, *Dalea candida*

- round stem
- hairlike stipules ◄
- alternate leaves
- circular simple leaves
  on young seedlings
- odd-pinnate
  compound leaves
  on older seedlings
- pointed leaflet tips ◄

4 CM

### SEEDLING DESCRIPTION

Leadplant emerges as a single stem.
The stem is round when rolled between
the fingers. Stipules located at the base
of the petiole where it joins the stem
are rust-colored and hairlike. Young
seedling leaves are alternate and almost
circular, with pointed leaf tips. As the
seedling matures, leaves change from
simple to odd-pinnate compound with
3–35 leaflets per leaf.

### LOOK-ALIKES

milk vetch: leaflike stipules
showy tick trefoil: hairy leaf margin

### GERMINATION AND GROWTH

Seed germination of leadplant is improved with moist-cold stratification.
This species grows in mesic to dry soils
and in full to partial sunlight. Leadplant
seedlings grow very slowly; 3 or more
growing seasons may be needed to produce flowering plants. Seed photo: hull
intact (top), hull removed (bottom).

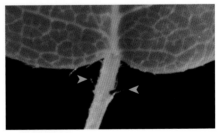

MM

0          3

7

- round stem
- hairlike stipules ◄
- alternate leaves
- serrated leaf margin
- glossy leaves

6 CM

### SEEDLING DESCRIPTION

New Jersey tea emerges as a single stem. The stem is round when rolled between the fingers. Hairlike stipules are located on the stem at the junction of the petiole. Leaves are alternate, glossy, and simple with serrated margins. Note: Because of the presence of stipules, this species was grouped with the legumes; however, New Jersey tea is in the buckthorn family.

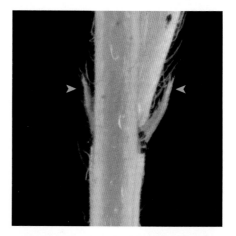

### LOOK-ALIKES

blue vervain: edged stem
Culver's root: opposite leaves
hoary vervain: edged stem

### GERMINATION AND GROWTH

Seed germination of New Jersey tea is improved by scarification followed by moist-cold stratification. This species grows in mesic to dry soils and in full to partial sunlight. New Jersey tea is a low-growing woody plant with several branching stems arising from a single taproot.

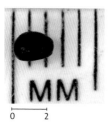

- round stem
- hairlike stipules
- alternate leaves
- compound leaf with 3–5 leaflets
- citrusy odor of crushed leaf
- pointed leaflet tips

### SEEDLING DESCRIPTION

Purple prairie clover emerges as a single stem. The stem is round when rolled between the fingers. Hairlike stipules are located on the stem at the junction of the petiole. Young seedling leaves are compound with 3 strap-shaped leaflets. Leaflet tips are pointed. As the plant matures, some leaves may develop 5 leaflets. Crushing a leaf produces a citrusy odor.

### LOOK-ALIKES

round-headed bush clover: hair prominent on the stem
white prairie clover: notched to rounded leaflet tips

### GERMINATION AND GROWTH

Seed germination of purple prairie clover is improved with dry-cold stratification. This species grows in mesic to dry soils and in full to partial sunlight. Purple prairie clover is a high-protein forage source for wild turkey, white-tailed deer, and quail. Seed photo: hull intact (top), hull removed (bottom).

5 CM

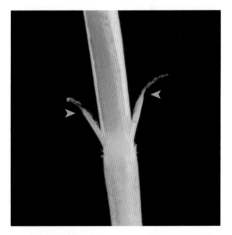

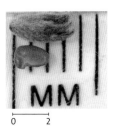

0    2

- round stem
- hairlike stipules ◄
- compound leaf with 3 leaflets
- pointed leaf tips ◄
- hairy stem and leaf margins

7 CM

### SEEDLING DESCRIPTION

Round-headed bush clover emerges as a single stem. The stem is round when rolled between the fingers. Hairlike stipules are located on the stem at the junction of the petiole. The stipules on young seedlings are light green, and darken as the plant matures. The first leaf is simple, and subsequent leaves are compound, with 3 leaflets. Each leaflet has a pointed tip that can be seen without a hand lens, making this species easy to identify. Hair is prominent on the stem and leaflet margins.

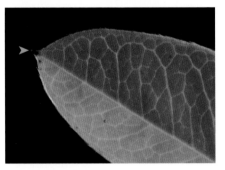

### LOOK-ALIKES

cream false indigo: leaflike stipules
purple prairie clover: straplike leaflets
white prairie clover: notched leaflet tips
white wild indigo: leaflike stipules

### GERMINATION AND GROWTH

Seed germination of round-headed bush clover is improved with moist-cold stratification. This species grows in mesic to dry soils and in full to partial sunlight. Dense, dark brown flower heads make round-headed bush clover easy to spot in the winter. Seed photo: hull removed.

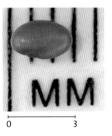

MM

0          3

- round stem
- hairlike stipules ◀
- alternate leaves
- circular simple leaves on young seedlings
- compound leaves with 3 leaflets on older seedlings ◀
- hair on leaf and leaflet margins

6 CM

### SEEDLING DESCRIPTION

Showy tick trefoil emerges as a single stem. The stem is round when rolled between the fingers. Hairlike stipules are located on the stem at the junction of the petiole and sometimes on the petiole near the base of the leaf. Young seedling leaves are simple and almost circular. As the plant matures, compound leaves develop, each consisting of 3 leaflets. Hair on the margin of leaves and leaflets can be easily seen with a hand lens.

### LOOK-ALIKES

flowering spurge: stipules absent
leadplant: pointed leaf and leaflet tips
milk vetch: leaflike stipules

### GERMINATION AND GROWTH

Seed germination of showy tick trefoil is improved with dry-cold stratification. This species grows in wet-mesic to dry-mesic soils and in full to partial sunlight. Showy tick trefoil's small, dark seed pods will stick to your clothes if you brush up against this species in the fall. Seed photo: segmented pod removed.

0       3

- round stem
- hairlike stipules ◄
- alternate leaves
- compound leaves with 3 leaflets on young seedlings
- notched and round leaflet tips ◄

5 CM

### SEEDLING DESCRIPTION

White prairie clover emerges as a single stem. The stem is round when rolled between the fingers. Hairlike stipules are located on the stem at the junction of the petiole. Young seedling leaves are compound with 3 leaflets. As the plant matures, each leaf can have up to 9 leaflets. Leaflet tips are notched or rounded. Crushed leaves of this species do not produce a citrusy odor.

### LOOK-ALIKES

cream false indigo: leaflike stipules
purple prairie clover: pointed leaflet tips
round-headed bush clover: pointed
    leaflet tips
white wild indigo: leaflike stipules

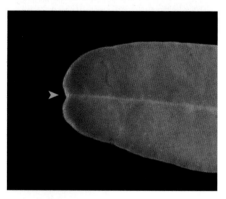

### GERMINATION AND GROWTH

Seed germination of white prairie clover is improved with dry-cold stratification. This species grows in mesic to dry soils and in full to partial sunlight. It is commonly called broom weed; Native Americans constructed brooms from its stems. Seed photo: hull intact (top), hull removed (bottom).

MM

0        3

# Forbs:
## Key Characteristic Group 2

Round stem, leaflike stipules,
alternate leaves

Cream false indigo, *Baptisia bracteata*

Milk vetch, *Astragalus canadensis*

Partridge pea, *Chamaecrista fasciculata*

White wild indigo, *Baptisia alba*

- round stem
- leaflike stipules ◀
- alternate leaves
- obovate, balloon-shaped leaflets ◀
- compound leaves with 3 leaflets
- hair prominent on stem and leaflets
- leaflets thick and fleshy when rubbed

### SEEDLING DESCRIPTION

Cream false indigo emerges as a single stem. The stem is round when rolled between the fingers. Leaflike stipules are located on the stem at the junction of the petiole. All leaves are compound with 3 leaflets, alternate, and connected to the stem with a very short petiole. Leaflets feel thick and fleshy when rubbed between the fingers. Hair can be seen easily without a hand lens.

### LOOK-ALIKES

round-headed bush clover: hairlike stipules
showy tick trefoil: hairlike stipules
white prairie clover: hairlike stipules
white wild indigo: hair absent on stem

### GERMINATION AND GROWTH

Seed germination of cream false indigo is improved with scarification followed by moist-cold stratification. This species grows in mesic to dry soils and in full to partial sunlight. Emerging shoots in spring look like asparagus. Cream false indigo seedlings grow very slowly; 3 or more growing seasons may be needed to produce flowering plants. Seed photo: color variants and pod removed.

4 CM

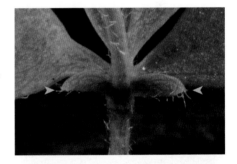

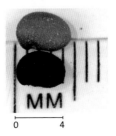

MM

0    4

- round stem
- leaflike stipules ◄
- alternate leaves
- odd-pinnate compound leaves with 3–35 leaflets
- oval leaflets with notched tips ◄

13 CM

### SEEDLING DESCRIPTION

Milk vetch emerges as a single stem. The stem is round when rolled between the fingers. Leaflike stipules are located on the stem at the junction of the petiole. Young seedling leaves are oval with notched leaflet tips and alternate on the stem. As the seedling matures, milk vetch leaves change from simple to odd-pinnate compound with 3–35 leaflets per leaf. Hair is easily seen on leaflet undersides but difficult to detect on leaflet tops.

### LOOK-ALIKES

cream false indigo: balloon-shaped leaflets
leadplant: hairlike stipules
showy tick trefoil: hairlike stipules
white wild indigo: balloon-shaped leaflets

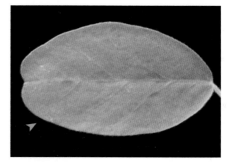

### GERMINATION AND GROWTH

Seed germination of milk vetch is improved with scarification followed by moist-cold stratification. This species grows in wet-mesic to dry-mesic soils and in full to partial sunlight. Large, leafy, shrublike plants and cream colored flowers make milk vetch easy to find in a prairie. Seed photo: pod removed.

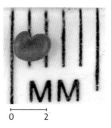

MM

0    2

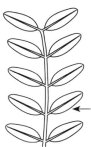

- round stem
- leaflike stipules ◄
- alternate leaves
- hair on stem and leaflet margins
- even-pinnate compound leaves with 8–24 leaflets
- pointed leaflet tips

8 CM

### SEEDLING DESCRIPTION

Partridge pea emerges as a single stem. The stem is round when rolled between the fingers. Leaflike stipules are located on the stem at the junction of the petiole. All leaves are even-pinnate compound with 8–24 leaflets, which makes this species very easy to identify at a young seedling stage. The first few leaves have 8 leaflets, and subsequent leaves may have up to 24 leaflets. Leaflets have a pointed tip. Hair on the stem and leaflet margins can be seen easily with a hand lens.

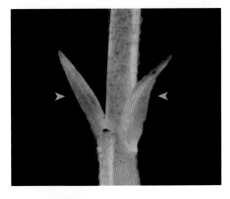

### LOOK-ALIKES

leadplant: hairlike stipules
milk vetch: notched and rounded leaflet tips

MM

0       5

### GERMINATION AND GROWTH

Seed germination of partridge pea is improved by scarification followed by moist-cold stratification. This species grows in mesic to dry soils and in full to partial sunlight. Partridge pea is an annual plant that grows rapidly and flowers in the first year. Seed photo: pod removed.

- round stem
- leaflike stipules ◄
- alternate leaves
- compound leaves with 3 leaflets
- balloon-shaped leaflets with notched tips ◄
- stem and leaflet hair absent

4 CM

### SEEDLING DESCRIPTION

White wild indigo emerges as a single stem. The stem feels round when rolled between the fingers. Leaflike stipules are located on the stem at the junction of the petiole. The first leaf is simple and balloon-shaped. Subsequent leaves are alternate, compound with 3 leaflets, and connected to the stem with a very short petiole. Leaflets feel thick and fleshy when rubbed between the fingers. Stem and leaflets are hairless.

### LOOK-ALIKES

cream false indigo: hair on stem and leaflets
round-headed bush clover: hairlike stipules
showy tick trefoil: hairlike stipules
white prairie clover: hairlike stipules

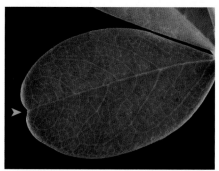

### GERMINATION AND GROWTH

Seed germination of white wild indigo is improved with scarification followed by moist-cold stratification. This species grows in wet-mesic to dry soils and in full to partial sunlight. Emerging shoots in spring look like asparagus. White wild indigo seedlings grow very slowly; 3 or more growing seasons may be needed to produce flowering plants. Seed photo: color variants and pod removed.

MM

0        4

# Forbs:
## Key Characteristic Group 3

Round stem, stipules absent,
alternate leaves

Flowering spurge,
*Euphorbia corollata*

Grass-leaved goldenrod,
*Euthamia graminifolia*

New England aster,
*Symphyotrichum novae-angliae*

White sage,
*Artemisia ludoviciana*

- round stem
- alternate leaves
- elliptic and oval leaf shapes
- very short petiole
- hairy stem and leaves ◄

### SEEDLING DESCRIPTION

Flowering spurge emerges as a single stem. The stem feels round when rolled between the fingers. Leaves are elliptic to oval, alternate, and connected to the stem with a very short petiole. Hair on the leaf margins and stem can be seen without a hand lens. This seedling has a unique appearance and is easily identified in the field.

### LOOK-ALIKES

leadplant: hairlike stipules
showy tick trefoil: hairlike stipules

### GERMINATION AND GROWTH

Germination of flowering spurge can be tricky. This species has a hard seed coat, and moist-cold stratification is needed to break seed dormancy. Flowering spurge grows in mesic to dry soils and in full to partial sunlight. Seedlings grow very slowly, and 2–3 growing seasons may be needed before flowering plants are produced. Seed photo: color variants.

10 CM

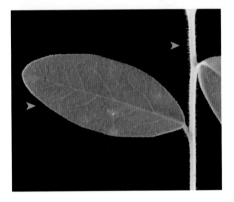

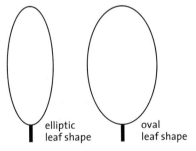

elliptic
leaf shape

oval
leaf shape

MM

0       3

21

- round stem
- alternate leaves
- 3 linear veins on leaves
- linear, straplike leaf shape
- sessile leaves ◄

7 CM

### SEEDLING DESCRIPTION

Grass-leaved goldenrod emerges as a single stem. The stem feels round when rolled between the fingers. Look closely at this seedling plant because there are some identification characteristics that can be easily missed. Leaves are strap-like, alternate, and connected to the stem without a petiole. Linear veins on the leaf surface resemble those of the grasses. Leaf margins have very small serrations that cannot be seen with the naked eye but make the leaf edges feel rough when rubbed across the fingers.

### LOOK-ALIKES

butterfly milkweed: opposite leaves
common mountain mint: opposite leaves
slender mountain mint: opposite leaves
prairie coreopsis: opposite leaves

### GERMINATION AND GROWTH

Seed germination of grass-leaved goldenrod can be improved by moist-cold stratification. To maximize light for germination, seeds should not be covered with soil after sowing. This species grows in wet to dry soils and in full to partial sunlight. Seedlings grow very slowly; 2–3 growing seasons may be needed before flowering plants are produced. Seed photo: color variants, pappus removed.

- round stem
- alternate leaves
- spatulate leaves
- leaves clasp stem ◄
- pubescent hairs on stem and leaves

6 CM

### SEEDLING DESCRIPTION

New England aster emerges as a single stem. The stem feels round when rolled between the fingers. Leaves are alternate and shaped like a spatula. Leaves are connected directly to the stem, clasping it without petioles. Short, soft hairs on the leaves and stem can be seen without a hand lens.

### LOOK-ALIKES

smooth blue aster: leaf petiole present
tall boneset: opposite leaves

### GERMINATION AND GROWTH

Seed germination of New England aster can be improved by moist-cold stratification. This species grows in wet-mesic to dry-mesic soils and in full to partial sunlight. In late summer to early fall, when most other prairie flowers have finished blooming, the rose-purple to purple flowers of New England aster glow in a planting. Expect flowering plants in the second growing season. Seed photo: color variants, pappus removed.

MM

0          2

- round stem
- alternate leaves
- serrated margin on less than half of leaf ◄
- stem and leaf hair prominent
- sage odor of crushed leaf
- whitish foliage

5 CM

### SEEDLING DESCRIPTION

White sage emerges as a single stem. The stem feels round when rolled between the fingers. Leaves are spatula-shaped and alternate. Less than half of the leaf is serrated. Leaves appear whitish from the hair on the leaf surface. Seen through a hand lens, the hairs appear matted and tangled on the leaf. As the seedling matures, the foliage takes on a whitish color and is easily recognizable. Crushing the leaf produces a strong sage odor. The leaf hair and sage odor are unique characteristics for this species.

### LOOK-ALIKES

None

### GERMINATION AND GROWTH

Seed germination of white sage can be improved by dry-cold or moist-cold stratification. To maximize light for germination, seeds should not be covered with soil after sowing. This species grows in mesic to dry soils and in full to partial sunlight. The unique white foliage of white sage makes up for its lack of showy flowers. Seed photo: color variants.

MM

0    2

# Forbs:
## Key Characteristic Group 4

Round stem, stipules absent,
opposite leaves

Butterfly milkweed,
*Asclepias tuberosa*

Culver's root,
*Veronicastrum virginicum*

Ironweed,
*Vernonia fasciculata*

Prairie phlox,
*Phlox pilosa*

Prairie sunflower,
*Helianthus pauciflorus*

Saw-tooth sunflower,
*Helianthus grosseserratus*

Swamp milkweed,
*Asclepias incarnata*

Tall boneset,
*Eupatorium altissimum*

## Butterfly milkweed *Asclepias tuberosa* | Asclepiadaceae, milkweed family

- round stem
- opposite leaves on younger seedlings
- straplike leaf shape
- very short petiole
- hair prominent on stem ◄

5 CM

**SEEDLING DESCRIPTION**

Butterfly milkweed emerges as a single stem. The stem feels round when rolled between the fingers. Leaves are oblong, opposite, and attached to the stem with a very short petiole. Leaves become alternate on older seedlings. Unlike other milkweeds, butterfly milkweed does not exude milky sap when leaves are crushed. Hair on the stem can be seen easily without a hand lens.

**LOOK-ALIKES**

common mountain mint: edged stem
prairie coreopsis: edged stem
slender mountain mint: edged stem
swamp milkweed: stem hair absent

**GERMINATION AND GROWTH**

Seed germination of butterfly milkweed can be improved by either dry-cold or moist-cold stratification. This species grows in mesic to dry soils and in full to partial sunlight. Butterfly milkweed is one of the few tallgrass prairie plants with a true orange flower. Seed photo: pod and pappus removed.

MM

0                    6

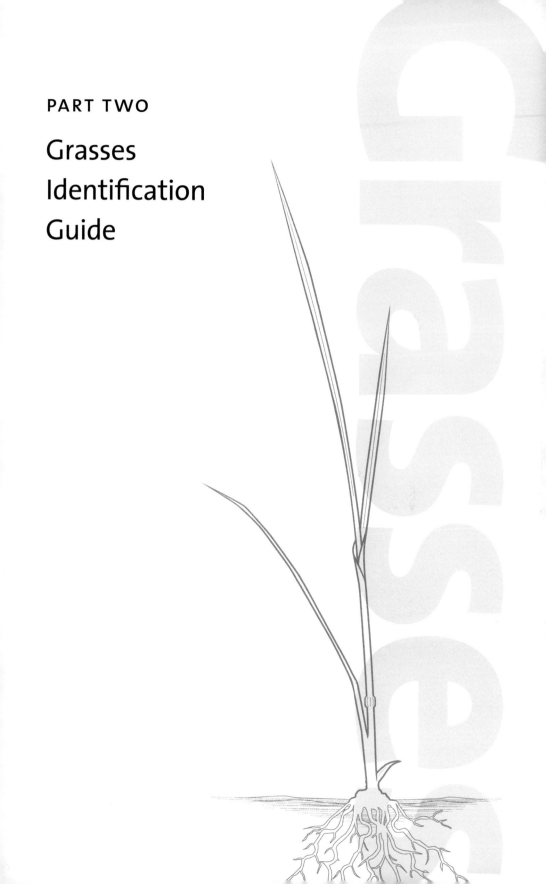

PART TWO

# Grasses
# Identification
# Guide

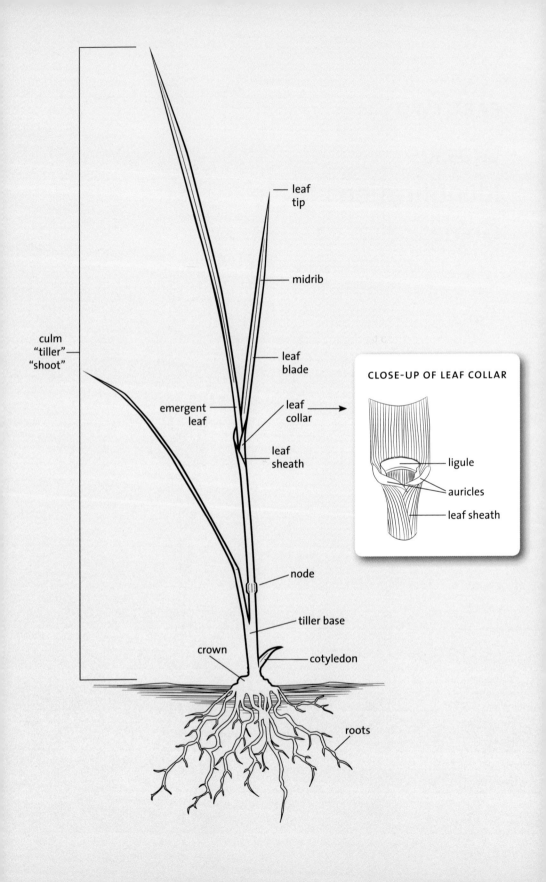

leaf
tip

midrib

culm
"tiller"
"shoot"

leaf
blade

emergent
leaf

leaf
collar

leaf
sheath

node

tiller base

crown

cotyledon

roots

CLOSE-UP OF LEAF COLLAR

ligule

auricles

leaf sheath

Welcome to the grasses identification section. Most prairie plants are perennial and grow slowly (above ground) in the first growing season. Therefore, plant identification may be easier when done in late summer after seedlings have had the most time to develop. Follow the easy steps below.

1. Roll the tiller near the base of the plant between your fingers to determine if it is flattened or round.
   a. Flattened tiller: go to key characteristic group 1, page 89
   b. Round tiller: go to step 2

2. Look for auricles connected to the leaf collar (a hand lens may be needed).
   a. Auricles present: go to key characteristic group 2, page 97
   b. Auricles absent: go to step 3

3. Look for hair on the leaf collar (a hand lens may be needed).
   a. Hair present: go to key characteristic group 3, page 102
   b. Hair absent: go to key characteristic group 4, page 111

# Grasses:
## Key Characteristic Group 1

Flattened tiller base, auricles absent

Big bluestem, *Andropogon gerardii*

Bluejoint grass, *Calamagrostis canadensis*

Indian grass, *Sorghastrum nutans*

Little bluestem, *Schizachyrium scoparium*

Side-oats grama, *Bouteloua curtipendula*

- flattened tiller base
- ligule with ragged top ◄
- coarse hairs on tiller and lower half of leaves ◄
- rolled emergent leaf

### SEEDLING DESCRIPTION

Big bluestem can be identified by its wide leaves, a tiller flattened near its base, and leaf hairs. The slight flatness can be felt by rolling the tiller near the base of the plant between the fingers. Coarse hair and a membranous, ragged top ligule can be seen without a hand lens. Hair is present on the tiller, the lower half of leaves, and leaf margins. By the end of the first growing season, some leaves may be blue to purple.

### LOOK-ALIKES

Indian grass: leaf hairs absent
little bluestem: folded emergent leaf
side-oats grama: swollen base of hairs
   on leaf margin

### GERMINATION AND GROWTH

Big bluestem is a warm-season grass, and seed readily germinates in late spring when soil temperatures warm to 55°F. Big bluestem grows as a sod-forming grass in ideal soil moisture conditions. In dry or wet soils, this species grows as a bunch-forming grass. Seed photo: hull intact (top), hull removed (bottom).

14 CM

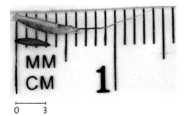

- flattened tiller base
- tall ligule with ragged top ◄
- swollen nodes on tiller ◄
- glabrous tiller and leaves
- leaf grabs finger when rubbed toward tiller
- rolled emergent leaf

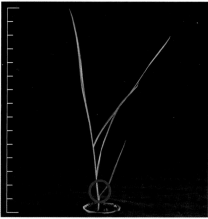

15 CM

### SEEDLING DESCRIPTION

Bluejoint has a unique ligule. It is tall and membranous with a ragged top that can be seen without a hand lens. The tiller base feels slightly flattened when rolled between the fingers. Leaves feel rough when rubbed toward the tiller. The tiller and leaves are nearly hairless.

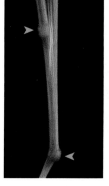

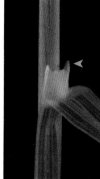

### LOOK-ALIKES

prairie cord grass: ligule of threadlike hairs

porcupine grass: tiller rounded near base

switchgrass: ligule a tuft of hair

### GERMINATION AND GROWTH

Bluejoint is a sod-forming cool-season grass, and seed germinates readily in early spring or fall when soil temperatures warm or cool to 39–45°F. Seed is very small and may need light for germination, so covering the seed with soil is not recommended. Look for this species in wetter soils. Seed photo: hull removed.

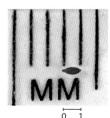

0   1

- flattened tiller base
- leaf hair absent ≺
- tall ligule stiff to the touch ≺
- rolled emergent leaf

### SEEDLING DESCRIPTION

Indian grass is most readily identified by the lack of hairs on its leaf and its stiff ligule. Leaves tilt away from the tiller, and the flatness of the tiller base can be felt by rolling it between the fingers. When a leaf is gently pulled back, the ligule can be seen easily without a hand lens. The notches in the tall ligule are sometimes described as like a rifle sight, and the ligule feels stiff when touched with a finger.

### LOOK-ALIKES

big bluestem: leaf hairs present
little bluestem: folded emergent leaf
side-oats grama: leaf hairs present

### GERMINATION AND GROWTH

Indian grass is a warm-season grass, and seed germinates readily in late spring when soil temperatures warm to 55°F. Indian grass is sod-forming and will readily establish and persist on mesic to dry soils. This grass develops a unique golden color in the fall. Seed photo: hull intact (top), hull removed (bottom).

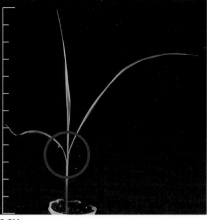

12 CM

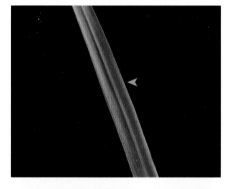

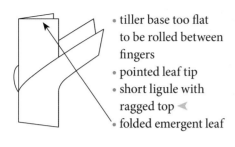

- tiller base too flat to be rolled between fingers
- pointed leaf tip
- short ligule with ragged top ◄
- folded emergent leaf

11 CM

### SEEDLING DESCRIPTION

Little bluestem seedlings are readily identified by their folded emergent leaf and very flat tiller. The emergent leaf is folded inside the tiller. Most other prairie grasses have a rolled emergent leaf. Near the base of the plant the tiller is so flat that it is almost impossible to roll it between the fingers. Little bluestem has a pointed leaf tip and a short ligule with a ragged top. This species is often confused with Kentucky bluegrass, but the leaf tip of Kentucky bluegrass has a keeled shape like a canoe and little bluestem has a pointed leaf tip.

### LOOK-ALIKES

big bluestem: rolled emergent leaf
Kentucky bluegrass: keeled leaf tip
side-oats grama: rolled emergent leaf

### GERMINATION AND GROWTH

Little bluestem is a bunch-forming grass that establishes well and persists in drier soils. Seed germinates readily in late spring when soil temperatures warm to 55°F. However, in well-drained loamy soils, little bluestem may be much less abundant when planted with the taller prairie grasses. Seed photo: hull intact (top).

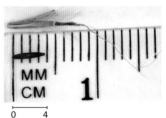

MM
CM     1
0     4

- flattened tiller base
- swelling at base of leaf margin hairs ◄
- hair on tiller and leaves ◄
- rolled emergent leaf

### SEEDLING DESCRIPTION

Side-oats grama has unique hairs on the leaf margins. They have a swollen, bulb-like appendage where they connect to the leaf margin, easily seen with a hand lens. The slight flattening of the base of the tiller can be felt by rolling it between the fingers. The underside of the leaf has a prominent keeled ridge. The ligule is short and membranous with fine hairs along its top.

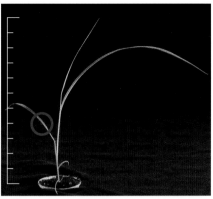

11 CM

### LOOK-ALIKES

big bluestem: no swelling at base of leaf margin hairs
Indian grass: leaf hairs absent
little bluestem: folded emergent leaf

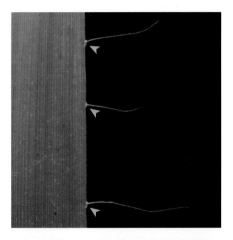

### GERMINATION AND GROWTH

Side-oats grama is a warm-season grass, and seed germinates readily in late spring when soil temperatures warm to 55°F. This species will establish and persist in drier soils when planted with taller warm-season prairie grasses, such as big bluestem, Indian grass, and switchgrass. However, in well-drained loamy soils, side-oats grama may decline over time when planted with these taller grasses. Seed photo: hull intact (top), hull removed (bottom).

# Grasses:
## Key Characteristic Group 2

Rounded tiller base, auricles present

Canada wild rye, *Elymus canadensis*

Virginia wild rye, *Elymus virginicus*

# Canada wild rye  *Elymus canadensis* | Poaceae, grass family

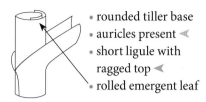

- rounded tiller base
- auricles present ◄
- short ligule with ragged top ◄
- rolled emergent leaf

## SEEDLING DESCRIPTION

Canada wild rye has a round tiller and, visible without a hand lens, distinct auricles projecting from the leaf collar. The ligule is short and membranous with a ragged top. Leaves feel somewhat smooth when rubbed between the fingers. Canada wild rye and Virginia wild rye seedlings are very similar.

## LOOK-ALIKES

Indian grass: flattened tiller base
Virginia wild rye: leaves rough when rubbed
switchgrass: ligule consisting of tuft of hair

## GERMINATION AND GROWTH

Canada wild rye is a cool-season grass, and seed germinates readily in early spring or fall when soil temperatures warm or cool to 39–45°F. Canada wild rye has a tendency to decline over time when planted with other prairie grasses. This species can grow in wet to dry soils and in full to partial sunlight. Seed photo: hull intact (top), hull removed (bottom).

14 CM

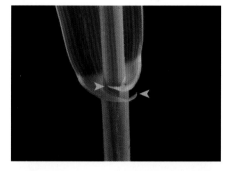

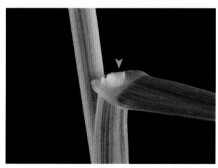

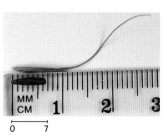

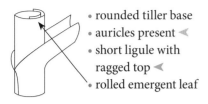

- rounded tiller base
- auricles present ◄
- short ligule with ragged top ◄
- rolled emergent leaf

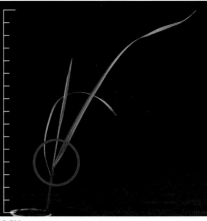

16 CM

### SEEDLING DESCRIPTION

Virginia wild rye has a rounded tiller and, visible without a hand lens, distinct auricles projecting from the leaf collar. The ligule is short and has a ragged top. A hand lens is needed to detect the very short hairs on the leaves. Leaves feel somewhat rough when rubbed between the fingers. Canada wild rye and Virginia wild rye seedlings are very similar.

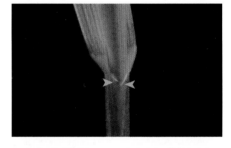

### LOOK-ALIKES

Canada wild rye: leaves smooth when rubbed
Indian grass: flattened tiller base
switchgrass: ligule a tuft of hair

### GERMINATION AND GROWTH

Virginia wild rye is a cool-season grass, and seed germinates readily in early spring or fall when soil temperatures warm or cool to 39–45°F. This species can grow in wet to dry soils and in full to partial sunlight. Virginia wild rye may be best suited to the somewhat shady conditions found in savannas and open woods.

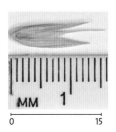

MM   1

0                    15

# Grasses:
## Key Characteristic Group 3

Rounded tiller base, auricles absent,
hair on leaf collar

June grass, *Koeleria macrantha*

Kalm's bromegrass, *Bromus kalmii*

Prairie cord grass, *Spartina pectinata*

Prairie dropseed, *Sporobolus heterolepis*

Switchgrass, *Panicum virgatum*

Tall dropseed, *Sporobolus compositus*

## June grass  *Koeleria macrantha*  | Poaceae, grass family

- rounded tiller base
- some hair on leaf collar margins, tiller, and leaves
- short ligule with ragged top ◄
- ribbing prominent on top side of leaf blade ◄
- rolled emergent leaf

### SEEDLING DESCRIPTION

June grass has a rounded tiller base. Some hair can be found on the tiller, leaves, and leaf collar. Leaves feel rough when rubbed from base to tip but smooth when rubbed from leaf tip to base. The emergent leaf is rolled.

### LOOK-ALIKES

Kalm's bromegrass: hairs prominent along leaf margins
little bluestem: flattened tiller base
side-oats grama: hairs with swollen base prominent along leaf margins

### GERMINATION AND GROWTH

June grass is a cool-season grass that germinates in early spring or fall when soil temperatures warm or cool to 39–45°F. Seed germination is improved with moist-cold stratification prior to seeding. This species grows well in dry soils and full sunlight. Seed photo: hull intact (top), hull removed (bottom).

12 CM

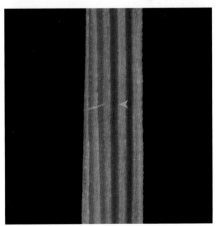

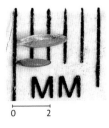

MM

0    2

- rounded tiller base
- pubescent hair prominent on tiller and leaf margins
- short ligule ◄
- rolled emergent leaf

### SEEDLING DESCRIPTION

Kalm's bromegrass has a rounded tiller base. Seedlings appear fuzzy from the abundant soft hair on the tiller and leaf margins. The ligule is short and membranous. Leaves feel soft when rubbed between the fingers.

10 CM

### LOOK-ALIKES

June grass: folded emergent leaf
little bluestem: folded emergent leaf
side-oats grama: flattened tiller base

### GERMINATION AND GROWTH

Kalm's bromegrass is a cool-season grass that germinates readily in early spring or fall when soil temperatures warm or cool to 39–45°F. This species may be best suited to the somewhat shady conditions found in savannas or open woods. Seed photo: hull intact (top), hull removed (bottom).

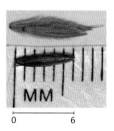

MM

0       6

- rounded tiller base
- some hair on leaf collar
- fringe of hairs for ligule ◄
- topside of leaf rough when rubbed toward tiller
- leaf and tiller hair absent ◄
- rolled emergent leaf

10 CM

### SEEDLING DESCRIPTION

Prairie cord grass can be difficult to identify when the seedlings are small. A close look with a hand lens is needed to find some hairs on the margin of the leaf collar. If the leaf is pulled away from the tiller, the ligule, consisting of a fringe of hairs, can be seen with a hand lens. Small serrations on the leaf margins make the topside of the leaf feel rough when rubbed toward the tiller. The underside of the leaf feels smooth when rubbed.

### LOOK-ALIKES

bluejoint grass: tall ligule with ragged top

prairie dropseed: hair prominent on leaf collar

tall dropseed: hair prominent on leaf collar

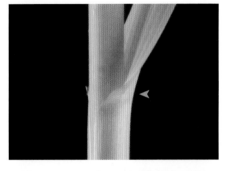

### GERMINATION AND GROWTH

Prairie cord grass is a sod-forming warm-season grass that germinates readily in late spring when soil temperatures warm to 55°F. This species grows in wet to mesic soils and in full to partial sunlight. Seed photo: hull intact (top), hull removed (bottom).

- rounded tiller base
- prominent hairs on leaf collar margins ◁
- long, thin, wispy leaves
- hairy tiller ◁
- leaf surface smooth when rubbed
- very small ligule with ciliate top
- rolled emergent leaf

### SEEDLING DESCRIPTION

Prairie dropseed has a rounded tiller base. Leaves and hair are very distinctive for this species. The leaves are long and thin, giving them a wispy appearance. The hairs on the margin of the leaf collar appear as a tuft that can be seen easily without a hand lens. Hair is prominent on the tiller but absent on the leaf. Leaves feel smooth when rubbed between the fingers.

### LOOK-ALIKES

bluejoint grass: tall ligule with ragged top
prairie cord grass: tiller hair absent
tall dropseed: tiller hair absent

### GERMINATION AND GROWTH

Prairie dropseed is a bunch-forming warm-season grass that germinates in late spring when soil temperatures warm to 55°F. Moist-cold stratification may improve seed germination. Long wispy leaves emerging from dense bunches make this species an ideal ornamental plant for landscaping. Prairie dropseed grows well in mesic to dry soils and in full or partial sunlight. Seed photo: hull intact (top), hull removed (bottom).

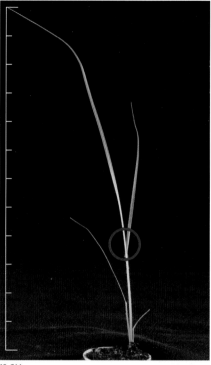

12 CM

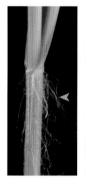
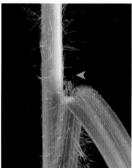

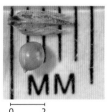

MM

0    2